CAESAR
AND
MAPANGA HOMESTEAD

ROSEMARY ARGENTE

© Rosemary Argente 2015

All rights reserved. No part of this book may be reproduced or transmitted in any form or by any means, electronic or mechanical, including photocopying, recording or by any information storage and retrieval system, without permission in writing from the author.

First edition 1982, titled *Caesar Tells The Story of Mapanga*
Second edition 2017

Cover: Cover, picture of Nipper, and text pictures
restored by Brian Sherman
Studio, Dumfries

Editor: Brian Sherman

ISBN: 978-0-9557327-6-8

Publishers: Asaina Books
Website: asainabooks.co.uk
Email: rosa@asainabooks.co.uk

Books by the same author:

Blantyre and Yawo Women
The Veil
The Promised Land - Companion to The Veil
Broken Temple
Praying Mantis
Difference
Share the Ride
Home From Home
Essays and Poetry
The Place Beyond
Caesar and Mapanga Homestead

Novels:
All Mine to Have
Farewell Sophomore
The Stream of Memory
A British Throne Scandal

Science Fiction:
Farewell to the Aeroplane

Booklets:
Journey of Discovery
Enduring Fountain - Health and Well-being
Katherine of the Wheel
Cooking With Asaina

Acknowledgements

My sincere thanks are due to Brian Sherman for editing the manuscript and for all his help with restoring old photographs and for supplying the photograph of Nipper. My thanks are also due to Ian Upton, David Duddle, Brian and Mark Sherman for their invaluable help on my struggles with technology.

CONTENTS

CHAPTER 1 1
CHAPTER 2 12
CHAPTER 3 15
CHAPTER 4 19
CHAPTER 5 25
CHAPTER 6 34
CHAPTER 7 38
CHAPTER 8 42
CHAPTER 9 45
CHAPTER 10 47
CHAPTER 11 50
CHAPTER 12 53
EPILOGUE 60

CHAPTER 1

Mapanga Lodge

I am a mixture of Alsatian and Rhodesian Ridge-back and they call us mongrel dogs.
I was born at Chirimba in a litter of several and I was three months old when Mama adopted me and took me to Mapanga. I lay on the passenger seat beside her and the smooth rocking sensation from the moving car sent me off to sleep. I woke to the sound of a voice calling me:
 "Come on, Caesar we're home!"
She lifted me from the car and set me on the ground. Sleepily, I surveyed my new abode—Mapanga Lodge, situated in the middle of a large estate on the eastern side of the looming Ndirande Mountain, and twelve miles from my place of birth.

The Lodge was a bungalow—what was normally called a house — of solid brick structure with walls that were fourteen inches wide, a tiled roof and worn window and door wooden frames that let in the biting June winds.
There was no mains water or electricity and paraffin lamps provided the lighting, what was in those days normally called 'hurricane lamps'; while a primus stove was the only means for cooking. Both items had little tanks at the base, for pouring in paraffin; the hurricane lamp was enclosed by glass where the wick peeped out from a centre opening in the little tank, and it had a handle. The primus had a single hob where to place a kettle or pot for cooking, and when lit, it had a single naked flame. Both, were lit by matches.

Our main water supply was from a 180 feet bore hole sheltered in a nearby pump house which yielded crystal clear

spring fountain water powered by an electric generator. The water was drawn in buckets and stored in 45-gallon drums in the kitchen area to cater for the entire household. There was no mains or piped water.
The Lodge was part of Mapanga Castle built in 1914 from a copy of a genuine castle in Italy as a private home, by one of the early Italian settlers, it was the only castle in eastern southern Africa.

On our side we had a splendid view of Ndirande Mountain in the west and in the east loomed Chiradzulu Mountain, whose hazy background was part of Mulanje Mountain, highest mountain in Malawi, of some ten thousand feet. The garden was wild, what a challenging playground, there were so many trees I wouldn't have a leg to stand on!

I was taken to the front verandah and introduced to a basket in which I was to sleep. The basket was made from bamboo by a local craftsman and it measured eight inches high and thirty inches diameter, with a little opening in the centre.
While Mama was out at work I had a wonderful game with my basket—so much more fun to play with. By the end of the week it was in shreds and I got a scolding for being so naughty. A second basket was brought which met with the same fate as the first and at the end of the third basked Mama gave it up as a bad job. Who wants to sleep in a silly basket when it's cooler and more comfortable on the bare floor?

After she had given me a bowl of bread and hot milk, which was to be my breakfast, Mama would speed off in her Volvo sports car to Blantyre, ten miles away where she worked and I would not see her until evening.
She left instructions with Eliza, wife of Steven, the builder, on the rest of my meals for the day.
I was given two main meals which consisted of the local

staple food 'nsima' made from *ufa*, maize meal flour, and this was mixed with meat and vegetables. I was also given light meals of fruit, custard and tit bits from Mama's table in between as I was taught to eat everything. Consequently, I grew to appreciate a varied diet, though bread remained my favourite item. The number of my daily meals were reduced to two and balanced as I grew older.

Other members in our homestead were artisans, the builder and two of his mates, who carried out extensive renovations to the Lodge. These consisted of replacing roof beams, and tiles with asbestos roofing material; fitting steel frames to the windows and doors—all were carried out while we were living on the premises. There was also a gardener and all of the workers went to their homes at the end of the day when a watchman came and stayed all night.

I was introduced to our friend, an ex Dragoon Guard (DG), who frequently came to have his meals with us and spent most of his spare time in the grounds of the Lodge with his spade digging away, terracing the grounds, laying out the gardens, or pruning the citrus trees. Somewhat jealous of him, though the jealousy was mutual, I took a great delight in chasing off his red Impala as he drove away. From then on I chased away every car that came to our house. Much as I was scolded, I could never get out of the habit of chasing cars until one day the rear wheel of a departing vehicle caught me full in the jaw and that put an end to my silly escapade.

"Where is everybody?" Mama asked me one evening when she found the place strangely quiet with nobody about except me. She called several times, before a paralytic figure staggered towards her. It was the watchman. The builder's mate had obtained some 'chibuku', local beer, passed it around, and all took French leave, including the watchman after he had related the incident. Could I have had a better opportunity to show my loyalty and devotion? I set myself on the front door mat and there I remained alert; every now and then I circled the house in watchfulness. This went on till Mama sorted out the staff problems and from then on all sorts of artisan concentrated on the completion in the refurbishing of the Lodge.

Plumbing was installed throughout the house, and the water supply came from the pump house close to the house. The garden was graced with rose bushes and a variety of shrubs and flowers.

Out of the blue Mama brought home two little bundles, honey coated, like me—a pleasant surprise! They were my sisters, Lulu and Cleo, from my mother's second litter. What a pal Lulu was. From the moment she arrived she cast an adoring eye at her big brother and we made a perfect team. But Cleo was rather shy and preferred to keep to herself. As Lulu grew older she became more vicious than I was in warding off the undesirable prowlers. As for the persistent trespasser I simply held him by the shorts while Lulu snapped at his calf! I'll always remember one occasion when a trespasser came along pushing his bike. I flew at him, he dropped his bike and in a flash he was up a nearby tree. After a while, he summed up enough courage and jumped down from the tree, picked up his bicycle, shouted some abuse at me and said:
    "I'll report these rabid dogs to the Vet!"

In our homestead we were surrounded by a variety of wild life which included monkeys, hyenas and jackals, not to mention the variety of snakes. The monkeys always returned every evening to sleep in the uppermost branches of the eucalyptus trees at the bottom of the cascading ground from the house. Early each morning they scattered away but it was when the guavas and mangoes were ripening in the numerous trees that they ventured close to the house. About a thousand yards away from our house and right in the middle of a thicket, there dwelt a leopard and her two little cubs.

Spiders abounded in many varieties, varying in size and beauty. They teemed on the footpaths and wove their strong silken webs from tree to tree. Perhaps the most beautiful was the small spider outstanding both in its beauty and by its skilfulness as an architect. In size it was as large as a five pence piece and it was shaped like an octagonal star. Its back was bright yellow with two red spots in the middle and eight points which covered the four pairs of legs also red. It built a diagonal web between several trees standing about six feet apart.

There were birds of feather in great varieties in our natural bird sanctuary and the air was filled with different kinds of bird song. But a more frequent and familiar song was that of the pied wagtail, the homestead mascot. He was black and white and had a long tail that wagged along, almost touching the ground and he often burst into fluty tunes, a comforting sound. The bee-eaters were supreme in rainbow plumage.
The ground horn-bill, a grotesque creature was another bird that announced the arrival of the rains. Scuffling along slowly and gravely, searching the ground for food. The hornbill is fetish and never killed by the people. In their sonorous, bell-like, rather monotonous sounds, pronounced alternatively in two different keys, the one an octave higher than the other, by the three or five individuals of which the party invariably consisted. It also has the gift of exciting dogs and when the dogs heard the characteristic voices of these birds they would shoot out barking hysterically at them. He had the gift of exciting us dogs, by flying so low but as we were about to

snap at him, he would fly high and away from our reach. Among these, one of the most frequently heard was the modestly plumaged Bulbul whose voice has been celebrated in oriental poems and songs. Its single sentence could hardly be called a song and yet there was a rare charm in it as it commenced with a cheerful trio and expired like a sigh in one plaintive, grave, and tender accent.

The commuting Carrion Crows were a domestic sight and were much more playful and freely entered into the spirit of sport with us dogs. They pretended to strike us, alighted on branches as low as they dared and gave utterances to a series of such queer and unwholesome sounds, unlike other bird song that give a pleasing orchestra to the ear. Of all bird sounds I would disqualify ravenal sounds, they certainly spoil the orchestra, a speciality of all ravens. We were delirious, barked frantically and engaged in the most unrestrained buck-jumps high up in the air in the hopes of snapping at the aggravating visitors. To show their utter contempt for these vain attempts the Crows assumed an attitude of supercilious disdain, and never budged an inch or moved an eyelid. Suddenly they would dive, just in front of your nose, and fly along the ground, provocatively slow and tantalizingly near; us dogs hotly pursuing them, then they would rise and settle in a nearby tree.
The Carrion Crow, a scavenger bird, is to be found in garbage dumps, they are protected by the municipality and it is illegal to destroy a Crow. The caw-cawing of the Carrion Crows at sunset as they flocked together on their homeward flight marked the end of a day. Unlike the crows of other land, seemingly they wore white collars. From early morning, the sweet melodies of low-flying and alighting birds around the place were replaced by the owl's song of a series of repeated hoots, starting from a deep loud note ending in a soft low note.

The awesome howl of the hyenas who were after cats or dogs for food were kept at bay by the barking of us dogs. In the background were far-distant wild animal eerie sounds, to which Mr Frog and his clan provided a croaking accompaniment; complemented by the human-baby like cries of that common dweller of the uppermost branches of the surrounding wild trees, and Jacarandas and Flamboyant: the night monkey, sometimes called the 'night baby', as the night was taken over by its unknown rulers.

Changa, Night Baby (also known as Night Monkey)

The experts from Oxford, England came and took pictures with a special torch at night of our little Changa (ChiChewa for night monkey or baby). The experts said they only saw two of the babies in our garden.

The other Changa

Lulu and Nero

Following the cacophony of these nocturnal sounds, each morning about three, preceding the bird songs, the 'orchestra of the lizards' would begin in a succession of squeaky notes followed by the sonorous conversations of the horn-bills, while the crowing of a cockerel, the voices of the wild doves heralded, in succession, the approach of dawn; and even the small birds were early risers and their half-drousy chirping was heard long before dawn. Our feathered friends of regular habits replaced the sun, particularly at night, as the most reliable substitute time-keepers. Though the Cuckoo is the earliest of all time keepers and starts about one o'clock after mid-night. The Cuckoo's are a series of coos like the whirl of a flying arrow and is repeated with increasing velocity until they culminate in one long-drawn vibrating note – one of the most characteristic notes of an African night.

When the *mpinimbi*, grape like fruit (not in clusters as grapes) had ripened on trees a pair of the fetish birds, the hornbill These two emissaries, after a stay of about a couple days, would disappear and in a short time a whole tribe of horn-bills would arrive and fill the place with their melodious screams, a blend of the braying of an ass and the bleating of a goat, much ear-ending shrieks.

The lizards were in abundance. They are found in warm climates and different areas of Africa. The large species have a blue body with a bright yellow head and a yellow stripe running along the back. They live in rocks and are rather shy creatures. The small type is more sociable and a common sight around the house.

The chameleons come in a range of colours and many have the ability to change colours according to the colour of their surrounding. They have rapidly extendible tongues; their eyes, particularly the large ones, are independently mobile but in aiming at a prey they focus forward in a coordination of a stereoscopic vision. They are adapted to climbing and visual hunting. Snakes also were found in the forest in their numbers and varieties, though we had one snake in a hole at the side of our house where she had her little ones. They never ventured beyond a tiny area of the garden surround of the house. They grew up and left, no doubt into the bush.

One morning when Mama was leaving for work there was a fat snake about 12 inches long in the driveway. As Mama got closer the snake woke up and was alarmed and stretched out to about 30 inches long as it headed for the bush. Sadly, the gardener killed it with such speed and Mama was upset. She said there was no point in killing it, or any animals, as it had harmed no one and the gardener had a puzzled look on his face! But snakes are not dangerous as they never go out of their way to attack anyone, unless accidentally trodden upon, which is very rare. It is rather sad that whenever one sees a snake the immediately reaction is to want to destroy it.

In the height of the dry season, the snakes sometimes went into houses or tents, in search of moisture or mice. It is extraordinary how well the village dogs knew from their earliest days how to distinguish snakes from other creatures. Whenever they saw a snake on the ground, they stood still, at first in silence and then bark but without going near it. One wonders if instincts not merely the memory of past incarnations which has been denied to man. If the snake happens to be moving in their direction, they give it a wide berth; if it is moving away from them they follow it at a distance while barking. They stand motionless when they see a snake in their awareness that makes, like lion bulls, and other large mammals, one constitutionally was disinclined to attack anything that faces them in perfect immobility. Nonetheless, a terrible thing happened. Cleo was bitten by a snake and she died almost instantly. For the bite of some snakes there is no cure. Lulu and I then realised that perhaps we had been hard on Cleo, although she was shy and was not one readily to join in any of our escapades. Looking back, it became apparent that without any intention on our part we had excluded her in our escapades. We regretted our callousness towards Cleo.

CHAPTER 2

Sometimes Lulu and I got carried away chasing guinea fowl for miles. We were severely reprimanded and Mama told us that the wild animals were our neighbours and we just had to learn to be neighbourly.
We had been at Mapanga Lodge for about a year when the house turned into a 'mini-mansion' with all modern amenities.

One day Mama got us pets together and told us a touching story. She said that long before our time, when sister Emma was a baby, she was given a dog, which she was reluctant to take because she thought of him as "ugly." She accepted the dog, and Rex, as she named him, proved himself. He was so loyal and was always at baby's side, protecting her twenty-four hours a day; and wherever Baby Emma went Rex followed beside her pram.
When Mama left to study in Britain, baby and Rex went to stay with granny in a new homestead, no more walks with baby and pram, and the other animals at the new homestead resented Rex.
Mama said while she was away she thought much about Rex and vowed to herself that she would make it up to him on her return. She took a boat on return home only to learn that Rex had died the day she
docked at the port of Beira. Rex hardly saw the baby, suddenly his life's interest ended, and he died of a broken heart at the prime of his life.

So, she went on:
 "Rex taught me that there is no such a thing as an ugly dog, or an ugly person. Dogs that fight or attack or maul people or

children have been conditioned by their owners to be that way. That there is no time like the present time; for we shall not pass this way again, and we must always try hard." Today is the story-telling day. Mama came up with another story in the days before sister Emma was born. In addition to their domestic pets, dogs and cats in the house she lived with her husband, Mama had two goats and one died giving birth to a fawn-colour kid. She obtained a baby bottle and strived to save the little kid and named him Bambi.

The orphaned Bambi - 1951

survived well and he grew up to be bigger than most goats but he became destructive in the garden, he ate the flowers and disrupted the flower beds.

Gray 1940

Sadly, he had to be given away. Mama also told us about her cat Gray. When Mama returned from her studies in England, Gray licked her face and sat on her lap. It was then she realised that cats were loyal too. Gray lived up to the age of 19.

Our days at the Lodge came to an end as we went to live in a ground floor flat at the blanket factory as tenants moved into the Lodge. The factory manufactured Kalulu blankets, and it was situated about a quarter of a mile away, with a splendid view of Ndirande Mountain from a different angle. From the silhouette of its elongated angle Ndirande was nick-named 'The Sleeping Warrior.'

CHAPTER 3

Kalulu
Kalulu means rabbit in the local ChiChewa language, a trade name for the blankets—soft, cuddly as a rabbit's coat. The Lancashire-made looms shuttled away, as one hundred weavers pressed on under supervision. There was much activity here as numerous business persons and traders called at the premises.

We had not been there long when someone brought a pretty little honey-coloured creature that had a pointed face and keen eyes. This little creature sat snugly in the palm of Mama's hand and I could have sworn it was a mouse. They named her 'Beaute'.
Beaute was the offspring of a snow-white Pomeranian sire and a pure black Toy Fox Terrier mother, and she looked like a honey-coloured Chihuahua. The cost of this precious little creature was just £4.
The thing that puzzled me most was that not only was Beaute allowed to live indoors but she shared Mama's bedroom in her little basket, and as the days went by she looked more like a Chihuahua. She never came outside on her own except by the side of the front door where Lulu loved to relax. There, the two of them would have a game which was quite something to watch. Beaute would pretend to attack Lulu in the face and playfully Lulu held Beaute's whole head in her mouth!

Beaute

Beaute was the most loving and lovable little creature and I do not think that a malicious thought ever entered her bright little head. She was exceptionally intelligent and certain words such as 'mouse', 'custard', 'tea', and many others were permanently fixed in her mind but her phrase for the undesirables, which she taught us all, was 'bad man'.

Beaute was up to all sorts of little prances and her physical energy was incredible, considering that she did not seem to have much interest in solid foods and a few drops of tea she took in the drawing room was her mainstay. But even then she regarded tea as more of a social event than anything else. A clatter of crockery meant that there was a cup of tea in the offing, accelerating her little prances. She sipped her tea from a tiny saucer. Sometimes she unbalanced herself and tipped into the saucer in a somersault!

She loved to play with a little solid rubber ring which measured three inches in diameter. The ring was tossed in the air and quick as lightning she caught it about two feet from the ground, quite a feat for a little scrap of a dog.

Beaute was obsessed by that ring of hers. She pestered all and sundry to have a game with her. When visitors came she would manifest her preference by placing the ring before the chosen guest, step back with her head inclined to one side, and prompted the guest to fling the ring in the air.

The status of this indoor dog continued to baffle me and I decided that I would try to overcome this terrible puzzlement so I took the bull by the horns, as the saying goes. I gallantly walked into the drawing room of the main factory residence where Mama was reading, with Beauty basking beside her on the settee.

"Hello Caesar!"

Mama greeted me rather cheerily. Beaute totally ignored me. I stood at the door unsure as to what I should do next. Then boldly, I ventured right in and said:

"I understand that now dogs are allowed indoors?" My question met with total silence.

I could not bring myself to occupy one of the upholstered chairs, so I said instead:

"I'll take a pew by the window", settling myself on the carpeted floor.

The continued silence was so thick that you could cut it with a knife but I further tried my hand at conversation:

"It is rather warm today, isn't it?"

"Oh! Rather," Mama replied. Then again total silence. I began to feel uncomfortable. After a short while I quickly got up and stepped outside.

Mama came out and found me relaxing under the shade of a tree in the garden and she said:

"Caesar, I think you understand."

"Yes, I do. My place is outside and I have no regrets", I assured her.

"Are you sure?" She went on.

"Certain", I replied.

"No hard feelings?" She pressed.
"No hard feelings", I affirmed and said:
"Besides, I do realise that I am a watchdog".

Then Mama took this occasion to say that:
"You know Caesar, dog is man's best friend. As I talk to you, I tell Beaute a lot of things and you can bet your bottom dollar that she would not tell on me." I understood her to say, she actually gossips with Beaute – fancy that...!
The next thing, Mama gets a cat named Snookie but the DG does not allow cats in the house. Snookie is in the habit of coming into the kitchen through the window and knows the difference between the DG and Mama, the latter always welcomes him in. One day Snookie is about to enter through the window and hears someone coming into the kitchen. He assumes it it the DG, attempts to retreat, but suddenly realises it was Mama and he somersaulted back into the kitchen!

Just as much as I was jealous of the DG, he was also jealous of me and I felt his resentment all along. One day one of the weavers came out of the factory into the courtyard at the front entrance to have a smoke and I flew at him. He ran back into the factory. The DG came out and I thought he was about to give me the usual scolding but instead he praised me:
"Well done, Caesar! That weaver is always looking for an excuse to dodge the work." Well, this was a surprise to me, though a pleasant one.
More renovations were carried out to the buildings surrounding the factory and at the end of four years the place had been turned into desirable executive premises when we again made another move. This time it was to the new 'Mapanga House', just a few yards from Mapanga Lodge.

CHAPTER 4

Mapanga Homestead

The house was built by the same builder who renovated the Lodge but under the supervision of a master builder. Most of his work mates and plus were engaged in the building. But would you guess where? Almost right on the spot where the leopard and her cubs once dwelt! Of course, they were no longer there, probably had moved closer to Ndirande Mountain. Most of the wild life remained the same as it was during our days at the Lodge. The house was not completed but liveable.

Here, a new challenge was presented to me. There was a stallion, Brutus and two mares, Jenny and Missy Lou; plus two cats, Lady and Ziggie; a large herd of Hereford cattle, and numerous Marino sheep in our new homestead set up.

A paddock for the cattle and sheep was built just beyond the Eucalyptus trees, abode of the monkeys, to the west of the house. Water was piped from the pump house and supplied to the drinking troughs built in and around the paddock. Temporarily, the horses lived in a separate field above and beyond the house closer to the main road.

Mama was kept busy organising various diet for the extended family of pets and livestock. Our farm cultivated and prepared our own cattle and horse feed, such as maize in the rainy season. Sweet potato and cassava were also grown without water in the dry season.

During the dry season, Lucerne, a highly concentrated cattle feed was grown. The produce was a useful supplement. Though some items, such as rock salt, molasses and *madeya* (maize husk), were bought from different suppliers. Mama could not take to feeding the animals with the meat and bone meal sold at the Cold Storage Commission - to feed meat to the herbivores goes against nature, she told us [later to be discovered as mad cow disease, in England!].

There was plenty of grazing for the livestock during the rainy season which covered the months of November to March. In addition, there was a vegetable garden with large quantities of cabbage which provided the essential greens for the horses in the dry season, and there were lesser quantities of carrots, other vegetables and legumes. The garden was watered by means of hose pipes and the water supply came from the pump house. The supplemental diet for the horses consisted of *madeya,* chopped cabbage, carrots, sweet potato or cassava, salt and molasses. The vegetables varied at times but next to the *madeya* the cabbage made up the main bulk of the mixture and Mama would not purchase the commercially produced horse ration, also for ethical reasons. For the

canine and feline pets, the quantity of home-made biscuits was increased. These highly concentrated, crunchy, more-some biscuits were handed out to us as tit bits. They were made from a mixture of ground peanuts (sometimes called groundnuts, home grown and dug from the ground), minced beef liver and *ufa* (maize meal flour), rolled, cut into rounds and baked in an oven on low heat until they were firm and slightly brown.

****

I felt that it was my duty to keep a watchful eye on everything and I commenced by helping to herd the cattle and sheep on their daily grazing away from the paddock. Sometimes I got carried away, my skin scratched and bleeding from the long elephant grass and rough ground in parts of the estate, and even nearly missed my dinner. I got some counselling from the 'Dhobi' (Ben Chitsonga, the household laundryman) who had served a previous family for over forty years and had come to join us in our homestead.

"Caesar, go to work if you wish but you must be in time for your
 dinner." He told me.

He was a wise and dependable character to have around. Each day, except Sundays, he ascended the cascade to carry out his duties which gave his immaculate touch to all the laundry of the homestead. Each evening he descended to his quarters beyond the paddock on the bank of the other side of the Lunzu River. Despite his repeated advice I seemed to be possessed and the attraction of herding the cattle and sheep was so great that I could not help myself. In the end Dhobi reported me to Mama and she forbade me to herd the livestock, and that was that.

"Caesar, in later life your body will suffer from this excessive chore you are placing upon yourself", she said.

There was a guest cottage at our homestead where numerous guests had come and gone. We had new guests, a couple named Tony and his wife Hilka with a little dog named Ricky. He was the most good-natured black terrier.

I overheard Tony tell Mama that while they lived in Beira, where they came from, there had been a mishap with Ricky and he never knew what was wrong, as he put it:

"I thought may be he had a fight or he was disappointed in love. There were no vets in Beira so I chartered a plane and took him to Salisbury (Harare) where the Vet discovered he had hernia and performed an operation upon him."

My, I thought to myself, I have never been in a plane before. Some dog Ricky!

Various works were carried out to the house and outbuildings as the concrete mixer chugged away. Overall supervising was Steven, the builder, and all sorts of artisans

assisting in his finishing touches to the drains, garden steps, terraces and sundry. Other members of the staff joined us in our expanding homestead: Hampton and Justin, the gardeners; Killion, supervisor of the livestock; and Juma, the groom for the horses. The horses were groomed in the mornings after breakfast and they grazed in the fields.
Late one afternoon the groom came running to the house with the sad news that Jenny had kicked Missy Lou to death. It appeared that Brutus and Jenny were attached to each other but to the exclusion of Missy Lou. We animals can be strange at times, and can be jealous of each other. From that day Mama had a block of stables built close to the house where horses could be kept in separate stables.

When the stables were completed there was much agitation as Brutus and Jenny were brought in and introduced to their respective stables. Brutus, placed at the end stable and casting an eye on Jenny in the next stable, declared his approval of the arrangement: This is is jolly."

In the days that followed we were enriched by various additions to our domestic scene though we were saddened by the exists of some of the members of our family.
On one morning there was a sudden scuffle and excitement around. Jenny had given birth to a filly but she was behaving strangely and was trying to kick her own baby.
The groom brought the filly into Dhobi's laundry room and Mama made her comfortable on a rug on the floor and called the Vet. Almost all day the Vet was with Jenny, doing his very best for her but to no avail and by evening she took her last gallop.
We mourned for Jenny and Brutus neighed for days, while his gaze was fixed in the direction he had last seen her. The loneliness he endured thereafter is indescribable.

The filly was such a sweet little thing, with dainty little hoofs. She was named 'Dainty', and she was fed from a baby's feeding bottle with slightly warmed milk and she was comfortably settled for the night. I was so deeply concerned about her safety that I made myself sentry at the door of the laundry room. Next morning I was greeted with:

"Oh, Caesar, what kind and selfless instincts you have. Watching over Dainty all night." Those were the words I loved to hear. But this was rather a hectic morning, sister Emma was leaving for her school in England.

Dainty - one hour old

Late Jenny's stable was made secure, for fear of the prowling hyaenas and leopards, and that was to be Dainty's stable. She was regularly fed on the bottle – after three weeks she consumed 33 pints of milk a day! As the days went by, she grew rapidly and became attached to Mama.

After a few days our Scottish vet telephoned to say that a post-mortem had revealed that poor Jenny had had rabies which meant that from then on the horses had to be inoculated against rabies like us dogs. Mama maintained a medical chart for each one of us animals to control the various inoculations we all had to have as they fell due at different times. The horses had to have tetanus toxide, and horse sickness injections; DHL for the dogs – the three in one injection; distemper for the cats and in addition to annual boosters of all these injections, all pets had to have a rabies booster annually.

One morning I espied a strange dog heading for Ricky. I flew at the attacker and he run away. Tony was telling Mama when she came home:

"Ricky was about to be attacked by a strange dog and Caesar, brave Caesar saved him. After which he began to lick Ricky, saying 'I am sorry, Ricky, I am so sorry.' "

Now, there is an animal lover I thought to myself.

CHAPTER 5

New Arrivals

A big truck pulled up at the house one afternoon bringing three more members to the domestic circle—Blasey, a chestnut mare, Bueno, a dark chestnut gelding; and Blackie, an Arab/Flemish gelding—ending the lonely days for Brutus. They had been collected from the railway station after their five-day journey from Southern Rhodesia. Four horses were supposed to come but one died on the way, for lack of water. Beaute stepped up to Bueno as her chosen one and placed her rubber ring before him, but he just gave her a couldn't careless look. The difference between them was about 500 pounds in weight!

The horses occupied their respective stables and each morning after their breakfast and grooming they were let out into separate fields to enjoy grazing and fresh air and perhaps a gallop if they were that way inclined. Usually during light drizzles of rain, they became accelerated, frisky, and boosted into little galloping sprees. About five o'clock, as the sun almost disappeared in the west, they hastened to their stables for the much-loved supper of *madeya* mixture and to bed.

Mama, out of all Robert Ragette's (Rouquette) grandchildren had a love for horses. The DG said "Mount and ride" and she did. How exhilarating as they rode through the ups and downs of the terrain of our area: cantering, galloping and jumping ditches, sometimes falling off! For us, the mongrels, it was fantastic following them along their trails. From then all sorts of visitors came to our homestead, particularly children who came to ride the horses for pleasure or take riding lessons from our friend, the DG.

Blasey

Blackie had been a race horse in Zimbabwe and Mama enjoyed her gallops with him. Another addition to the family travelled by plane from Zimbabwe in a little lemon coloured kennel: 'Little Grey Goblin of Bridport,' he was wearing a little blue knitted garment to keep him warm. When Mama took Goblin out of the kennel and held him, he pretended to bite her. When a dog pretends to bite you, he has accepted you – you're in!

He was a very highly strung little dog and supposedly brought over to be a companion for Beaute but she was so jealous of him at first. It was quite understandable considering that she had dominated the indoor scene up to that time and a new arrival was naturally considered a threat to her place. He was quite a little connoisseur—he loved to lick butter but if he was given margarine he would know the difference, and would not take it!

Beaute and little Goblin

It was rather sad in a way that for fear of Beaute's violence poor little Goblin had to hide under a chair when Mama came home in the evenings. Sometimes dogs, like children, can be cruel to each other.

Beaute's sadness is apparent in her face since little Goblin arrived
She was so jealous of him

No. C 20

Certificate of Pedigree.

NAME OF DOG LITTLE GREY GOBLIN OF BRIDPORT.
BREED CHIHUAHUA   SEX DOG   DATE OF BIRTH 2nd APRIL 1969
OWNED BY ROSEMARY ARGENTE   COLOUR GREY, WHITE SOCKS.
REGISTERED No. 220582   BRED BY MISS D. E. HADFIELD.
HONOURS WON BLANTYRE KENNEL CLUB - FIRST PRIZE

SIRE	GRAND PARENTS	G.G. PARENTS	G.G.G. PARENTS	
SIRE ROZAVEL EBANO OF BRIDPORT 174985 2 C.C.s	SIRE CHAMPION ROZAVEL MEXICAN IDOL	SIRE ROZAVEL EL PADRE	SIRE	CHAMPION ROZAVEL HUMO
			DAM	ROWLEY POLKA DOT
		DAM CHAMPION ROZAVEL UVALDA JEMIMA	SIRE	CHAMPION ROZAVEL HUMO
			DAM	UVALDA JOFOS MOOMIN
	DAM ROZAVEL HUASTECA	SIRE ROZAVEL MIGUEL	SIRE	BRANDMAN'S MODELO
			DAM	ROZAVEL LA ORA SENA DE ORA
		DAM ROZAVEL KARLENA'S BAMBI	SIRE	DON PANCHO VII
			DAM	ROSETTA III

DAM	GRAND PARENTS	G.G. PARENTS	G.G.G. PARENTS	
CHAMPION ROZAVEL PEDMORE WITCH MAGIC 174984	SIRE ROZAVEL WITCHDOCTOR	SIRE ROZAVEL EL PADRE	SIRE	CHAMPION ROZAVEL HUMO
			DAM	ROWLEY POLKA DOT
		DAM ROZAVEL BRUJA	SIRE	CHAMPION ROZAVEL HUMO
			DAM	ROZAVEL JOFOS ONLYONE
	DAM OLJON CARLOTTA	SIRE BELAMIE PEDAZO	SIRE	DENGER'S DON ARMANDO
			DAM	BELAMIE COSITA
		DAM OLJON TANNETTA	SIRE	BELAMIE DANDINO DALPASCA

BREED CHIHUAHUA   SEX DOG   DATE OF BIRTH 2nd APRIL 1969
OWNED BY ROSEMARY ARGENTE   COLOUR GREY, WHITE SOCKS.
REGISTERED No. 220582   BRED BY   MISS D. E. HADFIELD.
HONOURS WON BLANTYRE KENNEL CLUB - FIRST PRIZE

	GRAND PARENTS	G.G. PARENTS	G.G.G. PARENTS
SIRE ROZAVEL EBANO OF BRIDPORT 174985 2 C.C.'s	SIRE CHAMPION ROZAVEL MEXICAN IDOL	SIRE ROZAVEL EL PADRE	SIRE CHAMPION ROZAVEL HUMO
			DAM ROWLEY POLKA DOT
		DAM CHAMPION ROZAVEL UVALDA JEMIMA	SIRE CHAMPION ROZAVEL HUMO
			DAM UVALDA JOFOS MOOMIN
	DAM ROZAVEL HUASTECA	SIRE ROZAVEL MIGUEL	SIRE BRANDMAN'S MODELO
			DAM ROZAVEL LA ORA SENA DE ORA
		DAM ROZAVEL KARLENA'S BAMBI	SIRE DON PANCHO VII
			DAM ROSETTA III

	GRAND PARENTS	G.G. PARENTS	G.G.G. PARENTS
DAM CHAMPION ROZAVEL PEDMORE WITCH MAGIC 174984	SIRE ROZAVEL WITCHDOCTOR	SIRE ROZAVEL EL PADRE	SIRE CHAMPION ROZAVEL HUMO
			DAM ROWLEY POLKA DOT
		DAM ROZAVEL BRUJA	SIRE CHAMPION ROZAVEL HUMO
			DAM ROZAVEL JOFOS ONLYONE
	DAM OLJON CARLOTTA	SIRE BELAMIE PEDAZO	SIRE DENGER'S DON ARMANDO
			DAM BELAMIE COSITA
		DAM OLJON JANNETTA	SIRE BELAMIE DANDINO DALPASCA
			DAM BELAMIE TEHUANA

Signed D. E. Hadfield

Applications for Registration (fee R1.00/10/-) should be sent to the Secretary,
THE
KENNEL UNION OF SOUTHERN AFRICA
P.O. Box 562
Cape Town

RECORD OF PRIZES WON

26 August, 1972 BLANTYRE KENNEL CLUB
Class 1 - No. 1 - FIRST PRIZE

SALE OR STUD RECEIPT

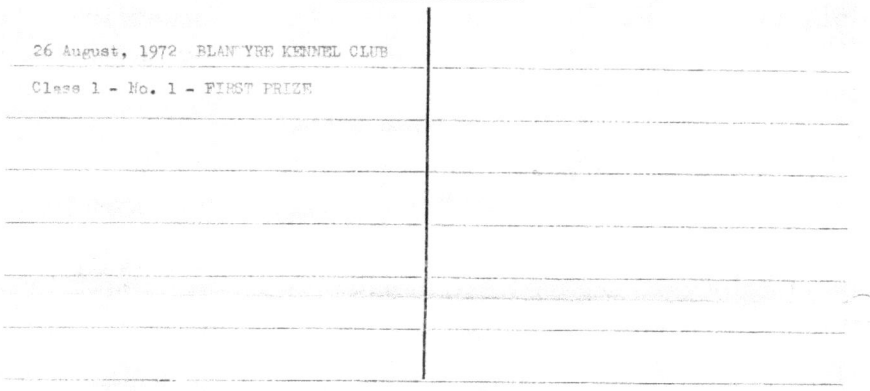

Received from Mrs Ashgate the sum of R/£ 60 for Little grey goblin

As they grew older they became closer but they were such little snobs! When they came out for walkies with Mama they would fly at Lulu and I, particularly Goblin, flinging his insults as if we had no right to be there. They were such minute beings that we just ignored them, though our turn came when Goblin and Beaute were obliged to stay indoors while Lulu and I followed on the horse rides through the estate, mostly on Saturdays and Sundays, up to four hours.

Mama knitted little garments for the little dogs to wear in the cold months. These garments had five holes in them. What were the holes for? Your guess is as good as mine!!

It was not long after her arrival when Blasey was in foal though we had to contain our excitement at the prospect of a newborn. The vet told us that mares had eleven months of gestation. Eleven months! Wow! Ages for us to wait for the great event. The day came. The vet was called, everyone waiting around. You should have seen the place. Everything seemed to stop in its tracks. The vet was with us for almost half a day.

Then finally, Blasey gave birth to a filly. She was named 'Tara' by our American friend, Mary, who regularly came riding. Tara was chestnut like both her parents and as she grew older she looked more like her mother though she had the blaze on her forehead as the sire, Brutus.

Tara

CHAPTER 6

Tragedy Strikes Again

Dainty was the tamest filly you ever knew. When she was called she neighed an answer and came galloping to the caller. At fifteen months old she was beginning to look like a mare. They put a head collar on her and a folded blanket on her back and she was lunged in the schooling field. There was great fun and excitement all round but I think Dainty enjoyed the fun mostly herself. One February afternoon, the horses were grazing in the fields when in the midst of soft rain there was a sudden clap of thunder which cracked a nearby tree and put the electricity out of order. The lighting that accompanied the thunder hit Dainty. The Vet was called but before he arrived Dainty was dead. The shock and loss to all of us was immense.

Dainty
Just before the tragedy

More New Arrivals of a different nature came to join us. Toing and froing with mud and soft grass, on the top of the lantern-style lamp suspended from the ceiling of the back verandah, entrance to the kitchen. Two swallows were industriously building their saucer-shaped mud nest on the top of the lantern. Their wings were blue-black, almost steely-blue; the throat and forehead of dark chestnut; and a buff breast. Their strong claws indicated adaptation to cling to upright surfaces, as they brought mud, straw, and feathers back and forth. On Saturday 14 August: their nest was completed and during the following three days the swallows brought soft feathers and fine grass for the interior furnishing of the nest. For three nights from the following Tuesday they both slept in the nest. While they were both out, Mama took a sneaky peak at the top of the nest without touching it and there were three eggs.

They both became very aggressive. For the next 33 days from the Saturday the mother alone incubated the eggs, while the father kept watch without; and he was very aggressive to anyone who came near the nest. In a motion of swifts, twists and turns accompanied by loud shrieks he would just miss striking the object in proximity, human or animal. He regularly brought and fed mother swallow with winged insects and she occasionally went out for very short spells leaving the father to keep watch. He could be distinguished from her by the two outside tail feathers, elongated into a graceful fork, which was apparent in the male.
After the end of fifteen days from the beginning of the aggression, three little heads with wide open little beaks could be seen taking insect food from the mouths of their parents, as they took turns in the 'meals on wings' service. Their mouths were lined with bristles made viscid by a salivating secretion, enabling the capture of insects in the open mouth. Most remarkable was the hygienic habit of the

little ones: they protruded their tails outside of the nest so their droppings could fall out of the nest to the ground – wildlife has rules of conduct and social organisation. On the twenty-eighth day from the feeding process mother swallow perched on the kitchen window sill and facing the nest enticed her brood to fly. In a succession of 'tweet-tweet' commands her young ones ventured out of the nest, fledgling, they perched on the telephone wires; now and again flying in and out of the nest and gradually extended the distances of their flights.

For the next three generations two of the offspring remained in the nest to commence and rear a family but always three eggs no more and no less. At the fourth generation one of them injured a wing and fell on to the cemented floor. Mama picked him up and mended his wing with light plaster and kept him warm and comfortable in the laundry room and fed him with grasshoppers and other winged insects. The name 'Ned' came to her mind. After two days she put Ned back into the nest. He completely recovered and resumed his flights of swifts and turns with his siblings. The little ones were fully grown and Ned could be distinguished from his two sisters by the two outside tail feathers, elongated into a graceful fork.

Towards the end of February a large gathering of swallows alighted on the gardenia bushes in the garden to a great *indaba* (conference). Ned and his family joined them twittering and chattering for half an hour; then all flew away. Night fell but Ned and his family did not return.

Swallows and Martins fly thousands of miles across the ocean twice a year during the winter and summer: Worcester, England, through Guernsey and Jersey to parts of Africa, some from Siberia to South Africa. They eat up to double their body mass in 24 hours of each day for 5 to 10 days before travel because they cannot eat and fly at the same time. They are a combination of an eating machine and flying machine, before they embark on their long flight across the ocean. To make provision for this combination, before and after flight, they reduce their digestive breast muscle and other organs become reduced as fuel. Emaciated they proceed on their flight. Too heavy with the intake of food to stop or land, dehydrated they build up their digestive system to take the combination as a prerequisite to the long distant flight.

Ned and his family had gone to Heaven only knew where. The nest remained empty for over a year.

CHAPTER 7

More New Arrivals

There were more new arrivals from Zomba, just up the road from us: A black Arab/Flemish gelding named 'Asher' and Shelley. Both horses were offered to us by a lady who said they belonged to her son, a young man of twenty-two who had committed suicide.
Asher had black and white socks, he was he most sweet natured and so beautifully schooled. It was such a treat to see him performing a dressage when mounted by the DG. Shelley, a Palomino mare, was also beautifully schooled but rather withdrawn and unpredictable. Shelley gave birth to a Palomino colt, sired by Brutus. He was named 'Kabul' by our English friend, John, but as sweet-natured Kabul grew older he became impossible. He broke gates and fences; trampled the flower gardens and on one occasion he actually raced off with a guest's hat! One day a little girl took him away to her parents' farm on Zomba mountain top.

Asher

From the airport Mama collected a little kennel containing two little travellers from Southern Rhodesia for a friend who named them 'Rajah' and 'Rani'. They were only in transit. They both came from Bridport, where Goblin came from, with their pedigrees. In fact, Rajah was the son of Goblin's sister. Rajah had a white coat with cinnamon patches and a sweet nature, not as highly strung as Goblin. Fully grown he weighed 5 lbs. Rani was the tiniest of them all. Her coat was white with black patches; her little face was beautifully marked; a black head with white eyebrows and a white muzzle. She was demure, like an Oriental queen, and she weighed just under 4 lbs. Rani soon gave birth to a son who was named 'Nawab' – prince. He had a pure white coat save for a little cinnamon patch below his right ear.

Nawab

Nawab's pedigree certificate presented a few problems. Detailed forms were sent to Johannesburg, South Africa, the nearest office for the registration of pedigree dogs. The forms were returned because they had been received in South Africa after Nawab had reached the age limit of three months prior to registration.

As soon as Rani arrived at Mapanga, on their frequent visits, she stepped out of the front door, surveyed all about her, and asserted her rights by her squeaky little bark—when a dog barks it's a sure sign of acceptance of a new homestead. At sunset, Rajah sat on the window sill and became, detached and pensive. No one could do anything to cheer him up but he was left to indulge in his solitude. When his mood had passed he readily and happily joined the others at play.

CHAPTER 8

Canine Idiosyncrasies

The canine have their little idiosyncrasies. When Rajah was not around, Goblin like the Sheikh he was, would step up to Rani: "Oh, Rani, delectable Rani..."

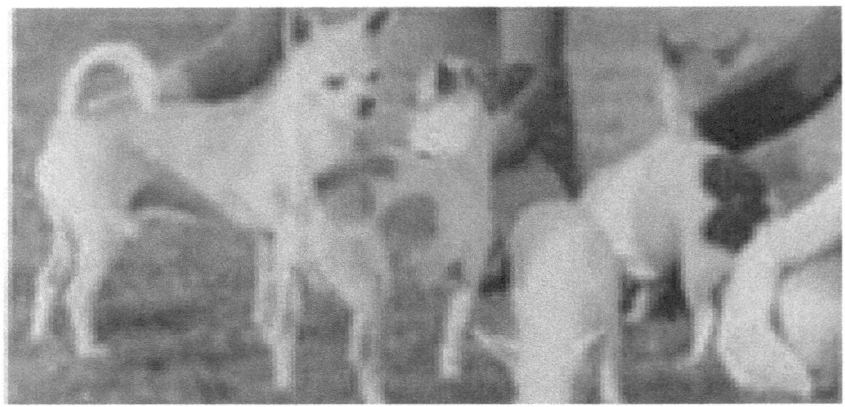

*Goblin (left) and Rajah
were always vying for canine supremacy*

But before he could finish, in a flash, Rajah would spring upon them:
"What's going on here?" And, Goblin would just slide off. Nawab, the happy-go-lucky, was everybody's pet and at 5 ½ lbs he was the heavy-weight. I do not believe that any bad thought ever entered his little innocent head. When Mama returned from work, the barking of all five at once was at its peak. Beaute was the self-appointed *kapitao* (captain), in her well-meaning efforts, to sort the others out, would come up with:
"Stop your nonsense, all of you, Mama is home!"

But the final word came from the smallest and firmest of them all, Rani. In the middle of it all Nawab developed billery and the Vet soon put him right. The additional aids such as wearing a tick collar, avoiding long grass, and special care, helped to keep this dreadful dog disease at bay.

The three of them often spent their holidays with us which made a total of five little yuppies in the house—there was never a dull moment.
Nawab had been bequeathed to us as a permanent member of our family. Now there were three of them indoors and Nawab blended and fitted into the stream of the family. They indulged in their play time within while Lulu and I barked at the prowlers without interrupting their indulgences. They would look up at each other questioningly:
   "What are the dogs barking at?"
They all loved music and dancing but Goblin was the champion of dance! At the sound of music and Mama's raised hands, he stood on his hind legs; his mouth in a snarl; his front paws flapping about in tune
to the beat of the music; while now and again glancing over his shoulder and proudly asserting to the others in body language:
   "Can you do what I can do?" Goblin's favouring tune was Neill Diamond's "Sweet Caroline".
To complement the occasion, Nawab would lay on his back, close his eyes in complete relaxation and in the anticipation for a human foot to tap on his tummy. Beaute just looked on. Another of their indulgences was car rides and when they heard the phrase: 'Mot-Mot', they went berserk, barking frantically while Nawab pretended to chew Beaute's ears and growling at the same time, giving her cauliflower ears.
The week-ends were particularly enjoyable as the venue for the games and relaxation was in our domain—Lulu's and mine: the garden! As pronounced by Beaute: "Gaarden."

As Nawab grew older, he and Goblin became great "gay pals" indulging fully. There was such scuffling around as they raced each other through the house in their varied escapades. Now, these things never bothered me, I was neutered when a puppy and I just looked on. This 'gay' state of affairs reigned until Beaute was in season when the two contestants entered into a boxing match which ended with Nawab losing a tooth! From then on Beaute transferred her attentions and affection to this very much younger suitor, Nawab—it was a case of loser takes all. No matter how hard Goblin tried, Beaute had eyes only for Nawab and the loneliness Goblin endured in the days that followed was painful to see.

CHAPTER 9

McNed Family

Then one Tuesday on 3 August after the long absence, a pair of swallows came along, back and forth with mud and soft grass busily engaged in renovating the existing abandoned nest. Then Mama called me: "Caesar, look! Swallows are building their nest on our verandah. This is a sign of good luck!"
We all watched in pleasant anticipation. The empty nest for over a year had somewhat become a source of sadness in our homestead. We all believed that Ned's progeny had returned and Mama named them 'McNed family.' Two of our new feathered friends had chosen to share our homestead. They may have migrated from Europe in their strong and vigorous flight. They were not unlike our previous friends in their characteristic traits...their saucer-shaped industrious labours on the top of the lantern. Like before, there were three eggs in the nest and they followed the same pattern in the incubation process.

****

The neighbour's hen and her seven chicks are free-ranging in our grounds, they enter by the torn parts of the boundary wire fence, and Mama says:
    "Let them be, they are our neighbours".
Oblivious to all else but ranging, they come every morning just after sunrise to leave in the evening ten minutes before sunset – daily during a period of four-weeks. Two chicks were lost in the process, sadly. On the fourth week mother hen did not accompany her chicks – they were old enough to fend for themselves, besides she was laying again. They

continued in their adolescence, as it were, free-ranging. How is that for mother hen?

Mother cat brought a mouse for her little one – how is that for a mother cat? Then Mother cat has had three more kittens. We watch them grow and two have been given away. The one Mama names Kita, a kind of short for Chiquitita stays on. She is rather wild, and needs taming. Mama gains her confidence with a piece of string dangling in front of her as she tried to catch it – she comes closer and she is given a saucer of milk. She grows bigger, today she climbed the curtains to get up to the open window.

****

CHAPTER 10

Tragedy Strikes, Yet Again

When Tara was six months old a terrible thing happened. It was about 4 o'clock in the afternoon, Blasey went through an opening in the wire fence leading to the main road and was hit by a motorcar. The driver of the vehicle got out of his car to see what had happened, he in turn was hit by an articulated lorry. The Vet was soon on the spot but there was nothing he could do. Man and horse lay side by side, dead.

During the burial of Blasey on the estate and thirty-six hours beyond, Tara and the other horses were left in the stables. When they were let out into the fields on the morning of the third day, Tara headed straight for her mother's grave where she dug with her hoofs and neighed pitifully. This went on for some days and then she attached herself to Bueno, who from then on became 'Uncle Bueno.' Horse instincts are incredible. Most people are not able to understand us, because we animals lack speech.

Uncle Bueno

Horse Idiosyncrasies are also something to watch. Brutus, as the only stallion, had his own field and lived apart from the other horses. Consequently, Tara had never come face to face with her father. Now and again Brutus got the impulse to crash the gates and head for the mares.
On one such occasion he headed for Tara and someone shouted:

"Brutus, that is your daughter!"

"I don't care whose daughter she is, I'm not fussy." He would say.

He was handled gently and escorted back to his field.
And, Tara, when she had spotted old Brutus for the first time has asked:

"Who is the old geezer?"

"Oh! That is your dad", replied Uncle Bueno.

Bleak was the evening when the telephone rang.

"I don't know how to tell you", it was Mama's friend.

"What has happened?" Mama asked.

"I have lost Rajah." She went on

"What do you mean?" Mama was surprised.

"He disappeared." She said.

Lulu and I were taken on leashes to pick the scent of Rajah and with some members of the staff we searched inch by inch of the area surrounding Rajah's home and vicinity but there was no sign of him. The broadcasting station, local newspaper advertisements and other means offering handsome rewards to the finder of Rajah,were put out. Mama's friend lamented:

"Wherever he is I do not know if he is cold or hungry".

The hours of searching turned into days but all in vain. After one week the intensive search was called off.

Then Mama brought a black Alsatian mongrel whom she

named Kim. The people who sold the dog advised her that Kim was essentially a watchdog; and that she should be kept chained during the day.
After a couple months Kim died suddenly and Mama believed that the cause was that she had been chained.

"You know Caesar, you cannot chain a dog. A young dog wants to romp about. After all, you were never chained, were you? Yet, you turned out to be a great watch dog. Kim has died of a broken heart." She said. I think this incident will haunt Mama for a long time, if not all her life.

Then, a most unusual thing happened. Mama brought a pair of mongrel puppies, brother and sister from one litter and they were named 'Nero' and 'Nefi'. They were a lovable pair with coats so light the Vet referred to them as 'yellow dogs'.
I had become so accustomed to the little Chihuahuas that I was puzzled at the arrival of two of Lulu's and my kind of breed. When I thought more seriously about it I realised that Lulu was becoming rather slow in her movements and she had been badly affected by arthritis. And, suddenly it also dawned upon me that little Beaute was not as frisky as she used to be and was rather weak on her legs. She could no loner jump on to the bed and a bed was prepared for her on the floor. About eight o'clock each night, in complete oblivion of her surroundings like an old granny, she would toddle off to bed—as she had become senile. They were growing old but what was I saying? Weren't we all? My back was not so good. I was feeling the old age myself.

CHAPTER 11

A Great Warrior Passes On

One morning, Blackie, the great racing warrior, was found lying down in his stable, most unusual. He had come to the end of the road. While waiting for the vet to arrive, Mama and the DG stayed with him in the stable. Mama tried to talk to Blackie, he raised his head slightly when he heard her voice, and looked at her but his head fell back to the ground. Just before the vet arrived Blackie took his last gallop. He was buried on the estate along with the other horses, calves and sheep that had departed before. The death of a horse is 'awesome' mingled with the sadness that comes with every death.

The groom, Juma, had departed after the death of Blasey. Because of his exceptional ability in looking after and handling the horses, Jonas the assistant groom had been specially trained to care for the horses, for the little dogs, and to keep an overall eye on all of us. He was outstanding in his natural love for animals and while Mama was at work, we were all secure and safe under his paternal care. He soon learned to prepare the little dogs' delicate diet which consisted of sauté beef, lamb or chicken, chopped finely and mixed with one third of vegetables and another third of boiled rice, making a total quantity of 2 and one half ounces for one meal for each dog.
They had lots of fresh water in between and cold milk in the evening though they always joined in the afternoon drawing room afternoon tea when Mama came home from work at the end of the day.
The diet of Lady and Ziggie of a mixture of either meat, fish or chicken with rice was a simple process in comparison.

Shelley, the Palomino mare, was as unpredictable as ever. When the mood took her, she would overthrow the rider. So the groom was instructed never to saddle Shelley for any visitor. One day the DG decided to ride Shelley, an experienced rider such as he was, Shelley failed to overthrow him, instead she took off in a mad gallop, one of the stirrups broke and DG fell. He fainted and was carried into the house. The incident was related to Mama when she returned from work.

****

Fourteen days from the day he disappeared Rajah's body was found not far from his home. It appeared he had received a fatal wound in the chest. Aged only five—thirty-five by human years—Rajah, a noble pet, died like a dog: murdered. But who would want to kill such an innocent and helpless little dog?
Strangely enough, soon after that, while on the lap of Mama's friend in a car, Rani, suddenly fell asleep—for ever.

I noted that when the little yuppies returned from their 'Mot-Mot' outings, poor little Beaute could not cope with all the excitement of springing out of the car—she tumbled to the ground and was trampled by the others in the scuffle:

   "Why do you allow these people to walk over me?" She would moan.
As it happened one morning—in broad daylight—a fox with a bushy tail attacked Nero and Nefi. Lulu and I flew at the fox in defence, and although we managed to ward off the attacker it was a great strain on both of us. I fully realised then why Nero and Nefi had been brought—to replace Lulu and me eventually.

As if to confirm my fears, Nero and I had a fight and I came off worse. This upset Mama very much:

"I am so sorry, Caesar, it was remiss of me to bring other dogs at this time." She did not expand but I knew what she meant... One Monday morning a messenger called at the house to tell us that "Dhobi" had passed away. Seven years short of his 100th birthday, he had faithfully reported for duty up to three days before his death.

CHAPTER 12

Twilight

This is Goblin, asked to finish this tale. My memory is not all that good. I am getting on you know. Twelve dog years equal eighty-four human years. Mama called us together and with our heads bowed we listened as she told us that Caesar was very ill and that we had come to the brink of a changing era.
Caesar refused to eat or drink anything and he wandered off into the garden where he lay in the shade of a gently swaying willow tree. He was found there cold and still. He was buried underneath the branches of that willow tree. About a couple months after that Lulu's arthritis became acute and she was taken to the Vet where she was put to sleep.

Then the most unexplainable thing happened. Mama left. Our constant friend, the DG, took care of us and we loved our evening walkies with him during which poor old little Beaute had to be carried. Three months short of her fourteenth birthday, the saddest day came when Mama received a cablegram, through sister Emma:

> "I was having my supper and the three little ones came to the dining room as always. Half way through the meal I passed a small piece of morsel under the table without looking. It was not taken from my hand, even when I called their names. I looked under, and there was little Beaute fast asleep, for ever, and she looked so lovely. Her eyes wide open and so clear. She is alongside Caesar..."

Nawab took it very hard and he could not understand. He refused to go for walks without Beaute and he would not eat. He sat on his haunches and pleaded: "Please, please, bring her back."

I became pensive at the sadness of life and I felt the loss very deeply, though my heart was broken before.

Au Revoir

Everything had changed so drastically. Lady, Ziggie and the cattle were gone and only a few of the sheep were left—they went different ways and most passed away.

The fields and grounds appeared massive in their apparent emptiness; departed were the children as they came no more to ride the horses – grown up and most probably with children of their own. Of the horses only Asher and Tara were left to grace the diminished homestead.

A few of the sheep were left

One day just out of the blue there was some agitation and excitement around the house as our DG invited Nawab and I to join him in the 'Mot-Mot' and we drove to the Airport to fetch Mama!

Asher

Of the horses Asher and Tara were left to grace the diminished homestead, and only one ewe was left. She was so attached to Asher and Tara that when a doctor bought Asher and Tara Mama's condition was that he took the ewe as well. He took them to Nkhoma Mission where he worked. After a few months he sent a letter to Mama asking for permission to put the ewe to sleep as she had became so aged and infirm.

Then, Nawab went for a holiday to his original home to visit Mama's friend, where he was attacked and mortally wounded by a wild cat. He died two days later and was brought to Mapanga to be buried beside Caesar. The DG and Mama were present.

Brutus was almost thirty years of age and suffering terribly from arthritis. He wandered off to what used to be the paddock at the bottom and lay in the meadow for some time. Then suddenly he gained momentum and slowly ascended the incline, pressing forward like a brave warrior, and made it to his stable.
Mama made the drastic decision to put Brutus to sleep and she called the vet. All our Scottish vets were no longer there, the new vet was from Holland and he used a little hand gun to shoot Brutus. Mama was upset – she would have preferred an injection...but the vet knew better. Asher and Tara neighed for Brutus, the great stallion of his time - no man or beast knows where, when, or how death would come.

Postcript:

Goblin had dementia and he went to stay in the home of Nawab. He never recovered from a second heart attack. Mama and DG went and collected him, and laid him beside Caesar. The DG was ailing and Mama took him away to her new found home at the confluence of the River Thames and Castle Mill Stream.

****

Thirty Years Later

It is hot dry, yet humid as always when the rains are brewing like most of Africa. What a variety of blossom on leafless trees, of different colours: red, purple, pink, yellow, orange, white and others beautiful beyond description, thriving on dust and dehydration – the speciality of Africa. Of greater quantity are the non-decidious trees of different shades of green: flamboyants, weeping willow, macadamia, cinnamon and others.

Birds love and live in trees and there are many of different plumage, still around Mapanga Homestead. The Jack Fruit, the cure for cancer, in its massive tree was still around. Its fruit was not unlike the custard apple though it has a foul smell, sometimes called 'crocodile fruit' for its rough skin. Other areas surrounding Mapanga homestead are void of trees and shrubs – all cut and used for firewood, the means for existence in all its abounding forms, but more particularly as a means of daily existence for the locals in cooking their frugal meals.

In the early morning I am disturbed by the sound of a baby crying piteously.

"Why is the baby crying, whose baby is it?" I ask.

"No, there is no baby here", replies the gardener. That is China, the old dog. All the other dogs have left him, gone to the bushes – he is so old he can't make it." Poor old China, youth has left him truly bereft. The more youthful dogs are six and a cat Chika with her baby, I named Butch. The animal idiosyncrasies are so fascinating where I am hosted, the home I established many moons ago. I am a guest at my own home, a total stranger. All so changed: gone are the cattle, sheep, horses, dogs and cats; not to mention the people who once worked or visited here – all passed away. I have been visiting, flying back and forth, and to get into the town centre, I pass through the same old road but how it has changed. On the left side is a dump site for the rubbish from the city centre. On the right side, all the trees towards the Sleeping Warrior have been cut.

The small graveyard is twenty times larger than its original size thirty years ago. I pass a squalid trading centre, where food items are displayed on a subsistence level, as a façade to shanty dwellings, flanking the main road: nuts, cassava, sweet potatoes, and the variety of fruit in abundance, mangoes, guavas, bananas, oranges, and others. The traders and buyers are in abject poverty and squalor at its height. Yet, despite this sad state of affairs, they are ever smiling and take a moment to exchange pleasantries with anyone – the true pleasant characteristic of the Malawian.

The weeping willows shed their cascading ever green leaves upon the grave of Caesar, super dog, protector, and defender of Mapanga Homestead: with Beaute, Goblin and Nawab surrounding him in eternal rest.

Thirty-seven Years Later

Author continues...

THOUGH ONE'S PETS MAY only live in memory, we can still enjoy other people's pets in our contemporary existence. One such is Nipper of Dumfries who was named after Nipper (1884-1895), the dog who served as a model for a painting titled His Master's Voice, by Francis Barraud's original painting of Nipper looking into an Edison Bell cylinder phonograph. The picture of the original Nipper was the basis for the dog-and-gramophone logo used by several audio recording and associated brands.

Nipper of Dumfries - Born 31st January 2017

****

EPILOGUE

The loyalty of dogs is second to none. It is said by some that dogs are loyal just because they depend on humans for food and shelter, but when you see how dogs react when their humans and canine friends come back after they have been gone for a long time, it becomes apparent that it is not just about food.

Dogs are also naturally affectionate. Immediately they meet their owner instinctively they want to bond. And they want to love and be loved. They want to be part of a pack and instinctively those who share a homestead are part of the pack in the dog's mind. Dogs are most loyal friends and constant companions – they just love you for what you are.

Researchers originally believed domestic dogs separated from their wolf ancestors after they began living among humans. More recent studies of the mitochondrial DNA of wolves and dogs show the two split about 135,000 years ago. Archaeological evidence on the discovery of buried dog bones near human settlements, suggests dogs and humans began sharing their lives only about 13,000 years ago. After the domestication of the dog, the two species developed an understanding that no other species shared with humans. According to Dr Stanley Coren *(The Intelligence of Dogs)*, studies have shown that dogs can tell the difference between selfish and generous humans.

All animals, domestic and wild, are part of our existence. They need our protection, and to be treated with kindness. Though we are brief tenants on this earth, in our life shared with our pets, we are surrounded by lives even shorter than ours.

A true story with photographs of domestic and wild animals on a homestead farm told through a dog, Caesar, who is the keeper and defender of the entire homestead in his wisdom and loyalty...he knew the perimeters of the homestead...from the moment he was set down when he arrived at Mapanga as a puppy, he resolved to look after the entire homestead and all who lived there, including guests. He tells of the inter relation between human and animal; that animals have feelings, passions, care for their young...that pets were essentially members of the family, and like babies, they were totally dependent... he also understood that wild animals were part of and shared the homestead...they were to be treated with compassion.

www.ingramcontent.com/pod-product-compliance
Lightning Source LLC
Chambersburg PA
CBHW070134100426
42744CB00009B/1836